World About Us

Rainforests

By Kate Bedford

Stargazer Books

© Aladdin Books Ltd 2006

Designed and produced by
Aladdin Books Ltd

**First published in the
United States in 2006 by**
Stargazer Books
c/o The Creative Company
123 South Broad Street
P.O. Box 227
Mankato, Minnesota 56002

Printed in Malaysia

Editor:
Rebecca Pash

Design:
Flick, Book Design
and Graphics; PBD

Picture Researchers:
Brian Hunter Smart
Rebecca Pash

Literacy Consultant:
Jackie Holderness—former
Senior Lecturer in Primary
Education, Westminster Institute
of Education, Oxford Brookes
University, UK

*Library of Congress Cataloging-in-
Publication Data*

Bedford, Kate.
   Rainforests / by Kate Bedford.
      p. cm. -- (World about us)
   Includes index.
   ISBN 1-59604-040-8
   1. Rain forests--Juvenile
literature. I. Title. II. World
about us (North Mankato, Minn.)

QH86.B378 2005
   578.734--dc22

                         2004058611

CONTENTS

Notes to parents and teachers

This series has been developed for group use in the classroom, as well as for children reading alone. In particular, its text on two levels allows children of mixed abilities to enjoy reading about the same topic. The larger size text (A, below) offers apprentice readers a simplified text. This simplified text is used in the introduction to each chapter and in the picture captions. This font is part of the © Sassoon family of fonts whose maximum legibility is recommended for early readers. The smaller size text (B, below) offers a more challenging read for older or more able readers.

Understory gloom

It is dark, hot, and very still in the understory because the canopy roof blocks out nearly all sunlight and wind.

A

◄ Brightly colored flowers attract insects.

There is little air movement in the understory, so plants that grow here rely on insects and birds to **pollinate** them.

B

Questions, key words, and glossary

Each spread ends with a question that parents and teachers can use to discuss and develop further ideas and concepts. Further questions are provided in a quiz on page 30. A reduced version of pages 30 and 31 is shown below. The illustrated "Key words" section is provided as a revision tool, particularly for apprentice readers, in order to help with spelling, writing, and guided reading. The glossary is for more able or older readers.

In addition to the glossary's role as a reference aid, it is also designed to reinforce new vocabulary and provide a tool for further discussion and revision. When glossary terms first appear in the text they are highlighted in bold.

 See how much you know!

How often does it rain in a rainforest and how much rain falls in a year?

What do monkeys and macaws use to help them hold on?

Which is the darkest and warmest part of the rainforest?

How do bats go to sleep?

Which rainforest animal can look in two directions at once?

Where in the rainforest do piranhas live?

What is the rainforest floor covered in and what lives there?

Why are rainforests being cut down?

Key words

Sunlight
Rainfall
Tropical

A

Emergent
Canopy
Understory
Branch
Trunk

Fungus
Recycle
Root

Glossary

Camouflage—To be disguised among the surroundings.
Decompose—To rot or break down into simple nutrients.
Ecosystem—All the living things in a particular environment and the way they work together.
Extinct—The total disappearance of a particular type of living thing on Earth.
Greenhouse Effect—The process by which the earth's atmosphere is warming up due to a build-up of carbon dioxide.
Nectar—A sweet liquid found in flowers.

B

Nocturnal—Creatures that are mainly active at night.
Nutrients—The most simple form of nourishment for living things.
Pollinate—When pollen is taken from one flower to another to make new plants.

What are rainforests?

Rainforests are dense, warm, wet forests, with huge trees. They are very special places. Over half the known animals and plants in the world live in rainforests, and new ones are being discovered all the time!

◀ This is a tropical rainforest. It rains here almost every day.

More than six feet (two meters) of rain falls in a tropical rainforest every year. It is a hot, wet, and steamy place with little variation in weather and no seasons. As a result, the trees and plants stay green and keep growing all year round.

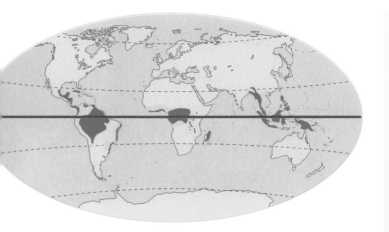

▲ The green areas on this map show where tropical rainforests grow today.

Most of the world's rainforests are tropical. They grow in "the tropics," a hot area just north and south of the equator. The equator is the imaginary line we draw around the middle of the earth. Some rainforests grow farther north and south of the equator where it is cooler. These are temperate rainforests. However, this book will focus on tropical rainforests.

◀ The yellow areas were once rainforests.

An area of rainforest the size of a soccer field is destroyed every second! They are cut down for their wood, or to make way for farms, mines, or roads. These unique and important environments— that affect the world's weather and provide us with medicine, food, and oxygen—could be lost forever.

 What is the weather like in a tropical rainforest?

Inside a rainforest

The heat and heavy rain in a rainforest are perfect for living things. Trees grow tall and flowers blossom. The lush rainforest provides food and shelter for the millions of creatures that live there.

◄ Rainforests recycle their own water.

Every day, the sun heats the rainforest, causing water from trees and plants to evaporate (turn into its gas form—water vapor). As the water vapor rises, it cools and condenses back into liquid water and forms rain clouds. When it rains, the plants soak up the rain and the **water cycle** begins again.

◀ **These vines climb up the trees to reach the sunlight.**

The rainforest is a complex **ecosystem** in which living things and non-living things, such as sunlight, interact. Every living thing in the forest depends on other plants and animals for food, shelter, or support, like these vines.

There are four layers in a tropical rainforest.

Each layer in the rainforest has different conditions. The animals and plants that live there have adapted to these conditions.

Emergent layer
Very tall trees have the most space and sunlight.

Canopy
The leafy treetops make a thick roof over the forest. Most of the rainforest wildlife lives here.

Understory
It is hot, shady, and very still.

Forest floor
Only a few plants grow in the dim light.

 Why do plants grow so well in a tropical rainforest?

Rainforest trees

Trees grow fast in the warm, wet rainforest. They race each other upward to reach the sunlight. Some trees grow much taller than others. They have long, straight trunks and their branches spread out wide at the top of the tree.

◄ **Some treetops are as big as a schoolyard.**

Huge trees, called emergents, can grow up to 230 feet (70 meters) tall! Their branches spread out over the forest canopy like an umbrella to make the most of the sunlight and space. They may also take advantage of the greater air movement at the top of the forest by developing winged seeds that can be carried by the wind.

▲ **Rainforest trees have large roots to prop them up.**

Rainforest trees have large "buttress" roots that spread out wide at their base like a skirt. They support the long trunk and anchor the huge tree firmly in place. The soil in a rainforest is shallow and **nutrient**-poor, so a tree's roots fan out wide rather than dig deep.

Monkeys live high up in the treetops.

Monkeys are excellent climbers and leap or swing between branches. They use their strong tail like an extra arm and coil it around branches to help them hold on. A monkey's tail has a bare patch under the tip, like the skin on the palm of a hand, to help it to grip tightly.

 Why do rainforest trees race each other upward?

Treetop life

Plants and animals crowd the treetops. Some plants don't need soil for their roots and many animals never touch the forest floor. The canopy provides all the sunlight, water, food, and shelter they need.

► **This three-toed sloth lives high up in the trees.**

Sloths are one of the slowest-moving creatures on Earth. They hang on to trees with hooked claws and spend most of their time asleep. Small plants called algae grow in their fur, turning it a greenish color. This helps to **camouflage** sloths from their predators.

▲ **This bush baby has large eyes to help it see in the dark.**

Bush babies are **nocturnal**. They spend the day sleeping in their nest and come out at night to feed on insects, fruit, and seeds. Their saucerlike eyes trap light, allowing them to see well enough to leap from tree to tree at night. Their long, bushy tails help them to balance.

Many plants grow on tree branches.

Plants known as epiphytes fasten their roots to tree branches without harming the tree. Some epiphytes have dangling roots that absorb water from the air. Other plants have leaves that form a bucket to catch water when it rains. Frogs and insects live in the pools of water they collect.

 Can you name some animals that live in the treetops?

High flyers

One-fifth of all the birds in the world live in tropical rainforests. They can be found, along with many other flying creatures, throughout the rainforest. They feed on insects, seeds, fruit, nectar, or other animals.

▶ **This bird lives in the treetops as part of a noisy group.**

Brightly colored macaws have short wings to help them fly through the crowded canopy. They have a powerful beak that they use as a tool to crack open nuts and fruits. Macaws also use their beak to hold on to the canopy branches as they move around.

This rainforest butterfly is the biggest in the world. ▼

Birdwing butterflies are poisonous, and their brightly colored wings warn other animals not to eat them. The poison in their bodies comes from a plant that they eat when they are caterpillars.

This bat feeds on fruit and nectar from flowers.

During the day, bats gather in large groups to sleep. They hang upside down from trees and sleep with their wings folded across their body. At night, they fly through the forest in search of fruit, insects, and **nectar** to eat. Bats are important to rainforest plants and trees because they **pollinate** flowers. They also help to spread seeds in their droppings.

 What do birds and bats feed on?

Understory gloom

Leafy bushes and small trees make up the understory. It is dark, hot, and very still here. The canopy roof blocks out most of the sunlight and wind from above. Many insects, frogs, and snakes live in this layer.

▶ **This is a chameleon. It can change its skin color.**

Chameleons camouflage themselves by changing color to match their surroundings. They use their long, sticky tongue to catch insects. They can also swivel their eyes so that each eye looks in a different direction at the same time.

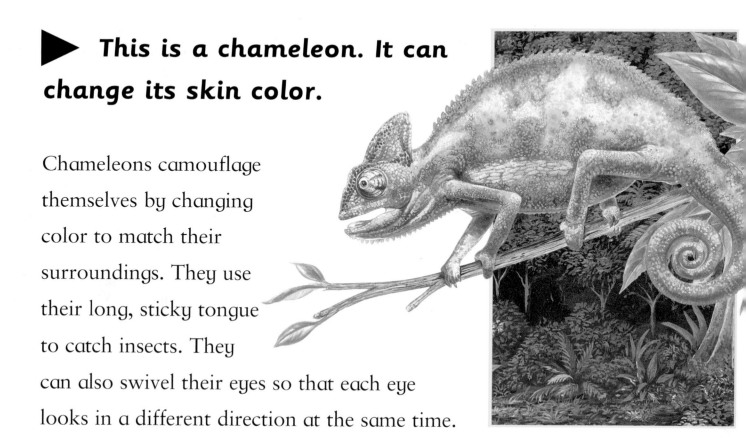

This passion flower is brightly colored to attract insects.

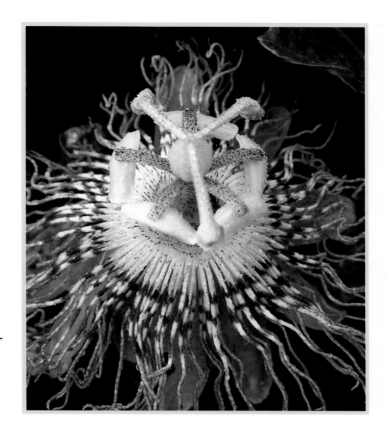

There is little air movement in the understory, so plants that grow here rely on insects and birds to pollinate them. To attract these animals, or pollinators, they often produce strong-smelling, colorful flowers that stand out in the gloomy understory.

This brightly colored frog has poisonous skin.

The brightly colored skin of the tiny poison dart frog acts as a warning to stop animals from eating them. Their poison is used by forest people on the tips of their hunting darts. Scientists are also developing the poison for medical purposes (see page 23).

 Why are some plants and animals brightly colored?

Life at ground level

The forest floor is the darkest and warmest part of the rainforest. Very little sunlight reaches the ground so few plants grow here. The forest floor is home to many insects and the animals that like to eat them, such as lizards!

► This huge rainforest spider is as big as a dinner plate.

The Goliath bird-eating spider is the largest spider in the world. It lives on the rainforest floor and hides in burrows or under logs during the day. At night, it comes out to hunt for lizards, frogs, insects, and small birds, which it bites with its poisonous fangs.

◀ **This jaguar's spotted coat helps it to hide when hunting.**

A jaguar's excellent sight, hearing, and smell, as well as its ability to climb and swim, makes it a great hunter. Jaguars usually hunt at dusk or dawn, when their spotted coat camouflages them in the dappled light. They catch animals such as monkeys, crocodiles, deer, and fish.

This rainforest fish is very dangerous.

Piranhas are small fish with razor sharp teeth that live in the rivers of the Amazon rainforest. They usually eat seeds and fruit that drop into the water, but sometimes they eat meat. In shoals, they hunt for animals that are swimming in the water. When piranhas attack an animal, they will eat everything but its bones in just a few minutes.

 Can you name some animals that like to eat insects?

Rainforest recyclers

The rainforest floor is covered with a thick layer of fallen leaves called leaf litter. Millions of insects, tiny creatures, and fungi help to break down the leaves. Anything that falls to the forest floor is not there for long!

▶ **Everything that falls to the ground is recycled.**

The hot, wet conditions in the rainforest are perfect for rotting, or **decomposing**. Insects and fungi help to break down dead plants and animals into simple nutrients. These are quickly absorbed by the shallow roots of trees and plants. Rainforests are so good at recycling that 99 percent of nutrients never leave the cycle!

▼ This rainforest fungus recycles dead animals and plants.

There are about 70,000 species of rainforest fungi. They come in different colors, shapes, and sizes— some even glow in the dark! Unlike most plants in the rainforest, fungi cannot use sunlight to make their food. Instead, they feed on dead plants and animals.

This termite eats wood!

Termites play a very important role in recycling rainforest nutrients. They break down 30 percent of the rainforest leaf litter. They are specially adapted so that they can digest cellulose, the material from which wood and plants are made. Termites live in huge colonies and build mounds from mud that can measure up to 18 ft (5.5 m) tall.

 Who are the rainforest recyclers?

Nature's superstore

Many of the things that we use and eat every day come from the rainforest. New animals and plants that could be useful in the future are being discovered all the time.

► **All of these things come from rainforest plants.**

Ginger

Brazil nuts

Cocoa pod

Coffee beans

Many of the foods that we eat come from the rainforest. Banana, coffee, and avocado plants first grew wild in rainforests and are now grown in large plantations. Some foods, such as brazil nuts, are still collected from trees growing in the rainforest.

The poison in these frogs' skin is being used to make a new medicine.

Scientists have discovered that the poison from the skin of this rainforest frog is an excellent painkiller. They have used the poison to develop a new medicine that is much safer to take than other painkillers. It is being tested and could soon be helping many people worldwide.

This rainforest plant has saved many lives.

This plant is a rosy periwinkle. It grows in the rainforests of Madagascar and is used to make a medicine for treating a disease called leukemia. Scientists have only looked for medicines in about one percent of the huge number of plants that grow in rainforests. They believe that many more life-saving medicines will be discovered in rainforest plants.

Which rainforest plants have so far become useful to us?

The earth's lungs

Rainforests only cover a small part of the earth's surface but they are sometimes called the lungs of the world. They help control the world's weather and affect the air we breathe.

► **Rainforests help to recycle gases in the air.**

Trees and other plants breathe in the opposite way to humans and animals. Trees breathe in carbon dioxide (which we breathe out), and breathe out oxygen (which we breathe in). This helps to balance gases in the air and ensures there is plenty of oxygen for us to breathe.

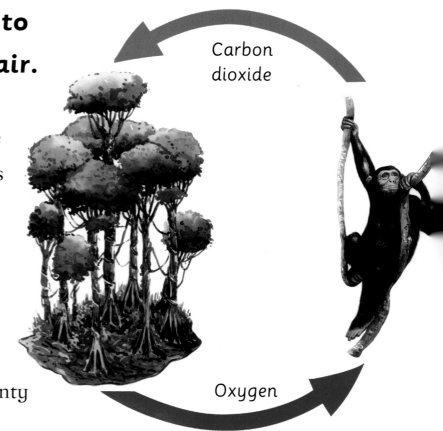

Carbon dioxide

Oxygen

▲ Rainforests soak up the heat from the sun.

Dark green rainforests absorb the heat and strong sunlight that shines in the tropics. When rainforests are cut down and more lightly colored vegetation grows instead, it creates a mirror effect. Sunlight and heat are reflected back up into the atmosphere causing it to warm up.

Cutting down rainforests is helping to make the earth warmer.

Carbon dioxide

When rainforests are destroyed, there are less trees to remove carbon dioxide from the air, so it starts to build up. Too much carbon dioxide in the atmosphere traps heat from the sun like the glass in a greenhouse. This is called the **greenhouse effect** and it is making the earth warmer.

 How do rainforests affect the air we breathe?

25

Homes under threat

People who live in rainforests know how to find everything they need. The forest gives them food, shelter, clothes, and medicine. In return, they treat the forest with great respect. They take only what they need, without causing any damage.

▶ **This man is weaving a roof using palm leaves.**

Rainforests throughout the world have been home to various tribes of people for thousands of years. They build their homes using rainforest plants and they hunt for meat, gather fruit and nuts, and grow useful plants in their gardens. They use the rainforest in a **sustainable** way that does not destroy it.

▲ **Rainforest is cleared to make cattle farms.**

Many people have moved into rainforests, but they use the forest in ways that destroy it. Huge areas of rainforest have been cut down to make way for farmland. But because the nutrients in the thin soil soon wear out, farmers move on to destroy new parts of the forest, leaving behind a bare, infertile piece of land.

This hillside was once covered in trees and packed with wildlife.

When a rainforest is cut down, plants, animals, and rainforest people lose their homes. Many species may die out and become **extinct**. Without the cover of the trees, the thin soil dries up and is washed away by the rain. The land is left like a desert and it is very difficult for rainforest to ever grow there again.

 How do rainforest people make use of the forest?

Rescuing the rainforests

Rainforests are important to all of us, so we must save them. Many groups of people raise money to protect and restore rainforests. The money might be spent replanting trees or teaching farmers how to look after the forest.

◄ **Growing crops in small patches helps to protect the soil.**

If local farmers learn to grow their crops in a similar way to the forest people, they can stop the thin soil wearing out. Growing patchworks of different plants and trees, instead of just one type, restores nutrients to the soil. Using the land sustainably means that farmers will not need to move on and cut down more rainforest.

◀ **People can visit this protected rainforest.**

Some rainforests have been turned into National Parks or reserves where it is against the law to cut down the trees. This helps to keep the animals, plants, and people that live there safe. Many tourists visit the parks to see the rainforest wildlife.

This gorilla could become extinct.

There are very few Mountain gorillas left because they have been killed by hunters and their rainforest home has been destroyed. To try and save them, the rainforest in Africa where they live is now a National Park. The money that tourists pay to see the gorillas is spent on protecting the rainforest.

 In what ways can rainforests be protected?

See how much you know!

How often does it rain in a rainforest and how much rain falls in a year?

What do monkeys and macaws use to help them hold on?

Which is the darkest and warmest part of the rainforest?

How do bats go to sleep?

Which rainforest animal can look in two directions at once?

Where in the rainforest do piranhas live?

What is the rainforest floor covered in and what lives there?

Why are rainforests being cut down?

Key words

Sunlight

Rainfall

Tropical

Damp

Hot

Emergent

Canopy

Understory

Branch

Trunk

Fungus

Recycle

Root

Glossary

Camouflage—To be disguised among the surroundings.

Decompose—To rot or break down.

Ecosystem—All the living things in a particular environment and the way they work together.

Extinct—The total disappearance of a particular type of living thing on Earth.

Greenhouse Effect—The process by which the earth's atmosphere is warming up due to a build-up of carbon dioxide.

Nectar—A sweet liquid found in flowers.

Nocturnal—Creatures that are mainly active at night.

Nutrients—The most simple form of nourishment for living things.

Pollinate—When pollen is taken from one flower to another to make new plants.

Sustainable—Methods that preserve and maintain, rather than destroy.

Water cycle—The process by which water is recycled over and over.

Index

Photocredits

Abbreviations: l-left, r-right, b-bottom, t-top, c-center, m-middle.
Front cover, 10tl, 12br, 13br, 19mr, 26br, 27tl, 27br, 28bl—Roger Harris/ www.junglephotos.com. Back cover, 3tl, 3mlb, 11tl, 12tl, 16tl, 21tr, 23bm, 29tl—Bill Perry-Behavior, Ecology, Evolution, and Systematics Section, Illinois State University. 1, 19tl—Gary M. Stolz/U.S. Fish & Wildlife Service. 2-3, 25t— Argentinian Embassy, London. 3mlt, 4ml, 5cb, 6ml, 11br, 14tl, 15tr, 17bl, 18tl, 20tl, 30mr— Klein Tours. 3bl, 5ct, 5bl, 6tl, 7br, 8tl, 15mr, 18br, 21bl, 29br, 30tr, 30br—Corel. 4bl, 17tr—Eléna Retsinas May. 6bl—Corbis. 9tl, 22tl—Flat Earth. 10bl— NASA. 14br— John Foxx Images. 15ml—Select Pictures. 17bl—Charles H. Smith/U.S. Fish & Wildlife Service. 22tr, 22c— Stockbyte. 22br—Keith Weller/USDA. 24tl— Corbis. 26tl—Gail Gillis/Explorations Inc. 28tl —Terence Freitas: Rainforest Action Network.